Cornelia Haas · Ulrich Renz

I0568678

My Most Beautiful Dream

Mein allerschönster Traum

Bilingual children's picture book

with online audio and video

Translation:

Sefâ Jesse Konuk Agnew (English)

Audiobook and video:

www.sefa-bilingual.com/bonus

Password for free access:

English: **BDEN1423**

German: **BDDE1314**

Lulu can't fall asleep. Everyone else is dreaming already – the shark, the elephant, the little mouse, the dragon, the kangaroo, the knight, the monkey, the pilot. And the lion cub. Even the bear has trouble keeping his eyes open ...

Hey bear, will you take me along into your dream?

Lulu kann nicht einschlafen. Alle anderen träumen schon – der Haifisch, der Elefant, die kleine Maus, der Drache, das Känguru, der Ritter, der Affe, der Pilot. Und der Babylöwe. Auch dem Bären fallen schon fast die Augen zu ...

Du Bär, nimmst du mich mit in deinen Traum?

And with that, Lulu finds herself in bear dreamland. The bear catches fish in Lake Tagayumi. And Lulu wonders, who could be living up there in the trees?

When the dream is over, Lulu wants to go on another adventure. Come along, let's visit the shark! What could he be dreaming?

Und schon ist Lulu im Bären-Traumland. Der Bär fängt Fische im Tagayumi See. Und Lulu wundert sich, wer wohl da oben in den Bäumen wohnt? Als der Traum zu Ende ist, will Lulu noch mehr erleben. Komm mit, wir besuchen den Haifisch! Was der wohl träumt?

The shark plays tag with the fish. Finally he's got some friends! Nobody's afraid of his sharp teeth.

When the dream is over, Lulu wants to go on another adventure. Come along, let's visit the elephant! What could he be dreaming?

Der Haifisch spielt Fangen mit den Fischen. Endlich hat er Freunde! Keiner hat Angst vor seinen spitzen Zähnen.

Als der Traum zu Ende ist, will Lulu noch mehr erleben. Kommt mit, wir besuchen den Elefanten! Was der wohl träumt?

The elephant is as light as a feather and can fly! He's about to land on the celestial meadow.

When the dream is over, Lulu wants to go on another adventure. Come along, let's visit the little mouse! What could she be dreaming?

Der Elefant ist so leicht wie eine Feder und kann fliegen! Gleich landet er
auf der Himmelswiese.
Als der Traum zu Ende ist, will Lulu noch mehr erleben. Kommt mit, wir
besuchen die kleine Maus! Was die wohl träumt?

The little mouse watches the fair. She likes the roller coaster best.
When the dream is over, Lulu wants to go on another adventure. Come
along, let's visit the dragon! What could she be dreaming?

Die kleine Maus schaut sich den Rummel an. Am besten gefällt ihr die
Achterbahn.

Als der Traum zu Ende ist, will Lulu noch mehr erleben. Kommt mit, wir
besuchen den Drachen! Was der wohl träumt?

The dragon is thirsty from spitting fire. She'd like to drink up the whole lemonade lake.

When the dream is over, Lulu wants to go on another adventure. Come along, let's visit the kangaroo! What could she be dreaming?

Der Drache hat Durst vom Feuerspucken. Am liebsten will er den ganzen Limonadensee austrinken.

Als der Traum zu Ende ist, will Lulu noch mehr erleben. Kommt mit, wir besuchen das Känguru! Was das wohl träumt?

The kangaroo jumps around the candy factory and fills her pouch. Even more of the blue sweets! And more lollipops! And chocolate!
When the dream is over, Lulu wants to go on another adventure. Come along, let's visit the knight! What could he be dreaming?

Das Känguru hüpft durch die Süßigkeitenfabrik und stopft sich den Beutel voll. Noch mehr von den blauen Bonbons! Und mehr Lollis! Und Schokolade!

Als der Traum zu Ende ist, will Lulu noch mehr erleben. Kommt mit, wir besuchen den Ritter! Was der wohl träumt?

The knight is having a cake fight with his dream princess. Oops! The whipped cream cake has gone the wrong way!

When the dream is over, Lulu wants to go on another adventure. Come along, let's visit the monkey! What could he be dreaming?

Der Ritter macht eine Tortenschlacht mit seiner Traumprinzessin. Oh! Die
Sahnetorte geht daneben!

Als der Traum zu Ende ist, will Lulu noch mehr erleben. Kommt mit, wir
besuchen den Affen! Was der wohl träumt?

Snow has finally fallen in Monkeyland. The whole barrel of monkeys is beside itself and getting up to monkey business.

When the dream is over, Lulu wants to go on another adventure. Come along, let's visit the pilot! In which dream could he have landed?

Endlich hat es einmal geschneit im Affenland! Die ganze Affenbande ist
aus dem Häuschen und macht Affentheater.
Als der Traum zu Ende ist, will Lulu noch mehr erleben. Kommt mit, wir
besuchen den Piloten! In welchem Traum der wohl gelandet ist?

The pilot flies on and on. To the ends of the earth, and even farther, right on up to the stars. No other pilot has ever managed that.

When the dream is over, everybody is very tired and doesn't feel like going on many adventures anymore. But they'd still like to visit the lion cub.

What could she be dreaming?

Der Pilot fliegt und fliegt. Bis ans Ende der Welt und noch weiter bis zu den Sternen. Das hat noch kein anderer Pilot geschafft.

Als der Traum zu Ende ist, sind alle schon sehr müde und wollen nicht mehr so viel erleben. Aber den Babylöwen wollen sie noch besuchen. Was der wohl träumt?

The lion cub is homesick and wants to go back to the warm, cozy bed.
And so do the others.

And thus begins ...

Der Babylöwe hat Heimweh und will zurück ins warme, kuschelige Bett.

Und die anderen auch.

Und da beginnt ...

... Lulu's
most beautiful dream.

... Lulus
allerschönster Traum.

The authors

Cornelia Haas has been illustrating childrens' and adolescents' books since 2001. She was born near Augsburg, Germany, in 1972. She studied design at the Münster University of Applied Sciences and is currently a professor on the faculty of Münster University of Applied Sciences teaching illustration.

Foto: Ingrid Hagenreich

Ulrich Renz was born in Stuttgart, Germany, in 1960. After studying French literature in Paris he graduated from medical school in Lübeck and worked as head of a scientific publishing company. He is now a writer of non-fiction books as well as children's fiction books.

Lulu also recommends...

Sleep Tight, Little Wolf

For ages 2 and up

with online audio and video

Tim can't fall asleep. His little wolf is missing! Perhaps he forgot it outside?
Tim heads out all alone into the night – and unexpectedly encounters some friends …

Available in your languages?

► Check out with our „Language Wizard":

www.sefa-bilingual.com/languages

The Wild Swans

Based on a fairy tale by Hans Christian Andersen

Recommended age: 4-5 and up

„The Wild Swans" by Hans Christian Andersen is, with good reason, one of the world's most popular fairy tales. In its timeless form it addresses the issues out of which human dramas are made: fear, bravery, love, betrayal, separation and reunion.

Available in your languages?

▶ Check out with our „Language Wizard":

www.sefa-bilingual.com/languages

ISBN **9783945174067**

Learn German with a fascinating story!

Would you like to read a fun story while getting serious instruction in grammar and vocabulary?

Then you should have a look at „Jens & Jakob" by Skapago Publishing. You can learn German with a coherent story that starts very simply, yet gets more and more advanced as the story progresses. Would you like to know how the story ends? If so.....you will just have to learn German!

For more information and a free preview see

www.skapago.eu

Do you like drawing?

Here are the pictures from the story to color in:

www.sefa-bilingual.com/coloring

© 2024 by Sefa Verlag Kirsten Bödeker, Lübeck, Germany

www.sefa-verlag.de

Special thanks to Paul Bödeker, Freiburg, Germany

Font: Noto Sans

All rights reserved. No part of this book may be reproduced without the written consent of the publisher

ISBN: 9783739960012